Who Can Solve the Crime?

Science Projects

Using Detective Skills

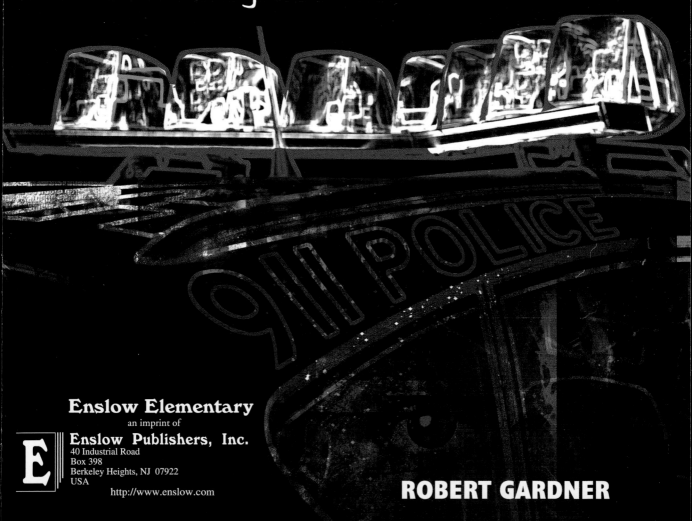

Enslow Elementary
an imprint of
Enslow Publishers, Inc.
40 Industrial Road
Box 398
Berkeley Heights, NJ 07922
USA
http://www.enslow.com

ROBERT GARDNER

Enslow Elementary, an imprint of Enslow Publishers, Inc.

Enslow Elementary® is a registered trademark of Enslow Publishers, Inc.

Library of Congress Cataloging-in-Publication Data

Gardner, Robert, 1929–
    Who can solve the crime? : science projects using detective skills / by Robert Gardner.
        p. cm. — (Who dunnit? Forensic science experiments)
    Includes bibliographical references and index.
    Summary: "Presents several science experiments using detective skills, such as observation, code breaking, and interpreting eyewitness evidence. Includes science project ideas and crimes to solve"— Provided by publisher.
        ISBN 978-0-7660-3247-7
        1. Forensic sciences—Juvenile literature. 2. Forensic sciences—Experiments—Juvenile literature. 3. Science projects—Juvenile literature. I. Title.
    HV8073.8.G39 2011
    363.25—dc22
                                                                        2008050062

Printed in the United States of America

052011 Lake Book Manufacturing, Inc., Melrose Park, IL

10 9 8 7 6 5 4 3 2

To Our Readers: We have done our best to make sure all Internet Addresses in this book were active and appropriate when we went to press. However, the author and the publisher have no control over and assume no liability for the material available on those Internet sites or on other Web sites they may link to. Any comments or suggestions can be sent by e-mail to comments@enslow.com or to the address on the back cover.

♻ Enslow Publishers, Inc., is committed to printing our books on recycled paper. The paper in every book contains 10% to 30% post-consumer waste (PCW). The cover board on the outside of each book contains 100% PCW. Our goal is to do our part to help young people and the environment too!

Illustration credits: Kenneth G. Rainis, p. 27; National Archives, p. 31; Shutterstock, pp. 7, 19, 28, 33, 35, 43; © Stephen Rountree (www.rountreegraphics.com), pp. 9, 18, 21, 32, 39; Wikimedia Commons, p. 16.

Cover illustration: Shutterstock

Contents

Who Dunnit?
Forensic Science Experiments

Experiments with a 🎖 symbol feature **Ideas for a Science Fair Project.**

Introduction

Crime scene . . . forensic evidence . . . fingerprints . . . DNA. You probably hear these words often. Forensic science television programs show scientists solving crimes. Perhaps you would like to try it, too! But what is forensic science?

Forensic science is the science used to solve crimes. The findings can be used in court. This means scientists have to be very careful when they collect evidence and investigate crimes. Evidence collected at a crime scene can put a person in jail. But some people have been found innocent and released from prison as a result of forensic evidence. In this book, you will learn about and practice some of the skills used by forensic detectives.

Entering a Science Fair

If you have to do a science fair project, doing one about forensic science can be lots of fun. Some experiments in this book are marked with a 🎗 symbol. They are followed by ideas for science fair projects. But judges at science fairs like experiments that are creative. So do not simply copy an experiment from this book.

Expand on one of the suggested ideas. Or think up a project of your own.

The Scientific Method

Scientists try to understand how things work. They make careful observations. They do experiments to answer questions. Nearly all scientists use the scientific method. They (1) observe a problem; (2) form a question; (3) make a hypothesis (a best-guess answer to the question); (4) design and do an experiment to see if the hypothesis is true; (5) analyze the results of the experiment; (6) if possible, form conclusions; (7) accept or reject the hypothesis.

Scientists often share their findings. They write articles telling other scientists about their experiments and results.

How do you begin a project you can use in a science fair? You start by noticing something that makes you curious. So you ask a question. Your question might arise from an earlier experiment, something you saw, something you read, or for another reason.

Once you have a question, you can make a hypothesis—a possible answer to the question. Once you have a hypothesis, you need to design an experiment. The experiment will test your hypothesis. For example, suppose your question is "Do fingerprints fade away in sunlight?" You would place one set of prints in the sun, and one set in the dark. Both sets should be kept at the same temperature, be made on the same surface, and so forth. Sunlight will be the only difference between the two groups.

During the experiment, you would collect data by observing the prints. Does either group of prints start to fade? Does either group begin to change in any other way? You might take photographs of the prints on a daily basis. You would compare the data collected from the two groups over a few days. You might then be able to make a conclusion.

Your experiment might lead to other questions. These questions will need new experiments. That's the nature of science!

Safety First

To do experiments safely always follow these rules:

1 Always do experiments under adult supervision.

2 Read all instructions carefully. If you have questions, check with the adult.

3 Be serious while experimenting. Fooling around can be dangerous to you and to others.

4 Keep your work area clean and organized. When you have finished, clean up and put materials away.

Detectives: Keen Observers with Sharp Senses

When police reach a crime scene, they first try to help any victims and, if possible, arrest suspects. Then they seal off the area. This prevents any evidence from being removed or disturbed. Soon detectives and forensic scientists arrive. They wear gloves and pull booties over their shoes. This protective gear prevents new fingerprints, footprints, and other bits of misleading evidence from contaminating the crime scene.

Detectives at a crime scene wear gloves so that they do not disturb evidence or add their own fingerprints to the scene.

1-1 Being a Keen Observer

Forensic teams observe a crime scene very carefully. They take photographs of the scene and any evidence they find. They make detailed notes, measurements, and drawings. They have to be sure of the location of all objects.

A careful search is made for evidence. The evidence might include a victim, a weapon, blood and other sources of DNA, hair, fibers, teeth marks, tool marks, glass, paint chips, bullets, fingerprints, and more. After going over the evidence, a detective becomes a scientist. He or she will form a hypothesis about the crime. The hypothesis must explain the evidence using sound reasoning. But a good detective, like a good scientist, must keep an open mind. A different hypothesis might also explain the evidence. And it might lead to a different conclusion.

Are you a keen observer? Let's find out.

1 Look closely at the drawing in Figure 1.

2 Make a list of all the irregular things you observe in the drawing.

3 What do you see that suggests a crime took place?

THINGS YOU WILL NEED:

- Figure 1
- notebook
- pen or pencil
- your home

Figure 1. Is this a crime scene? What observations might make you think it is?

4 What additional evidence would you look for and collect?

5 When you have finished, compare your list with the one on page 44.

How keen an observer were you?

Suppose a detective observed some of the photographs and other objects in your home. What would he or she know about you and your family?

 ## Idea for a Science Fair Project

Design, make, and play a forensic science board game. The game should require observation of clues to solve a crime.

How Careful Observation of Evidence Solved a Crime

Claire Josephs was murdered in Bromley, England in 1968. There was no evidence of a break-in, and coffee and cookies were on a table. Therefore, police believed Claire knew her killer. While interviewing friends as possible suspects, a detective noticed scratch marks on the hands of Roger Payne, a man that Claire knew. Police decided to investigate further. Using ultraviolet light, they found 61 red wool fibers on one of Payne's suits. The fibers matched those in the dress that Claire Josephs had been wearing when she was killed. Claire's raincoat hung on the inside of her front door. Police found 20 rayon fibers on the coat. The fibers matched fibers from Payne's scarf. He had probably hung his scarf over her raincoat. On the floor of Payne's car, police discovered fibers that matched carpets in the Josephses' home. They also found bloodstains there that matched Claire Josephs' blood type. Payne was found guilty of murder and sentenced to life in prison.

1-2 A Crime Scene Investigation

Pretend that your living room, family room, or bedroom is a crime scene. You are the detective.

1 Using a magnifying glass, search the floor, furniture, and other surfaces for "clues." You might find hairs, fibers, dirt, bits of paper, insects, etc.

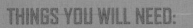

THINGS YOU WILL NEED:

- living room, family room, or bedroom
- magnifying glass
- forceps (tweezers)
- envelopes
- pen or pencil
- notebook
- an adult
- microscope (optional)

2 Use forceps to put the evidence you find in separate labeled envelopes.

3 Make notes and sketches of where you find things.

4 If you have pets, you may find dog or cat hairs as well as human hairs. If possible, ask an adult to help you look at these hairs under a microscope. By comparing the hairs you found with samples from you and your pets, you may be able to tell which hairs are human and which are from pets.

Can you match human hairs with the human from whom they came?

Can you match fibers you found with the clothes or articles from which they came?

Can you identify any insects you found? How about bits of paper?

Idea for a Science Fair Project

With an adult's permission, insert a new vacuum bag in your family's vacuum cleaner. Then vacuum the "crime scene." What visible evidence did you not observe the first time? What additional evidence can you find using a magnifying glass? Using a microscope?

🎗 1-3 "Observing" by Touch, Sound, and Smell

Detectives often use senses other than their sight. How well can you use your senses of touch, sound, and smell?

1 Find a large container such as a clean, plastic dishpan.

2 Put a number of things in the container. You might include the following: a tennis ball or baseball, a bar of fragrant soap, a toy doll, a baby's rattle, a bell, an orange, an apple, a plastic jar, a rubber band, a pencil, an eraser, a wad of paper, a plastic drinking straw, and other objects that are not sharp or dangerous.

3 Ask a partner to sit at a table. Put a blindfold on that person. Be sure your partner can't see.

14

4 Place the container with the objects you collected on the table in front of your partner.

5 Tell the person that the container holds a number of objects. Ask the person to try to identify each object using smell, touch, or sound. How successful was he or she?

6 Ask someone to prepare a similar object-filled container when you are not present.

7 That person will blindfold you. Then it will be your turn to identify objects by touching, smelling, or listening. How successful were you?

Ideas for a Science Fair Project

• Do girls do better than boys when identifying objects by touch, smell, or sound? Prepare an experiment to find out.

• Does age affect a person's ability to identify objects by touch, smell, or sound? Do an experiment to find out.

Sherlock Holmes: Keen Observer with Sound Reasoning

Sherlock Holmes, a fictional detective, gives us an example of keen observation and sound reasoning. In one story, Holmes says to his friend, Dr. Watson, "I see you are not going to buy South African stocks." Watson wonders how Holmes knows that.

Holmes explains:

> You had chalk on your left thumb and fingers last night. So I knew you were playing billiards. You only play with Mr. Thurston. You said a month ago that Thurston gave you an opportunity to buy South African stocks, but that the opportunity would last for only one month. Your checkbook is in my locker. You haven't asked for the key in more than a month. The opportunity to buy the stock has passed. You have seen Thurston, but you have not paid him any money. Therefore, you are not going to buy the stock.

Real detectives don't have authors to create an organized set of clues. They have a lot of evidence that may not make any sense. They often have to connect observations and facts that, at first, seem unrelated. But those connections can't be made without keen observations and facts that need to be connected.

By using a magnifying glass, a detective may see something she might otherwise have missed. By photographing a crime scene, a detective may see something he overlooked earlier. By talking to other detectives and forensic scientists, other observations and facts may come to light, and new hypotheses about a crime may emerge.

Sherlock Holmes, right, and Dr. Watson

Who Dunnit? A Crime to Solve: A Note Is Found

THINGS YOU WILL NEED:
Figure 2

A local bank was robbed on October 28. A citizen found a crumpled piece of paper near a sidewalk. He opened it but could not read the strange writing. The writing is shown in Figure 2. He took it to the library and showed it to the librarian who called the police. As the police department's detective, you have been asked to examine the paper.

What do you conclude?

What would you do next?

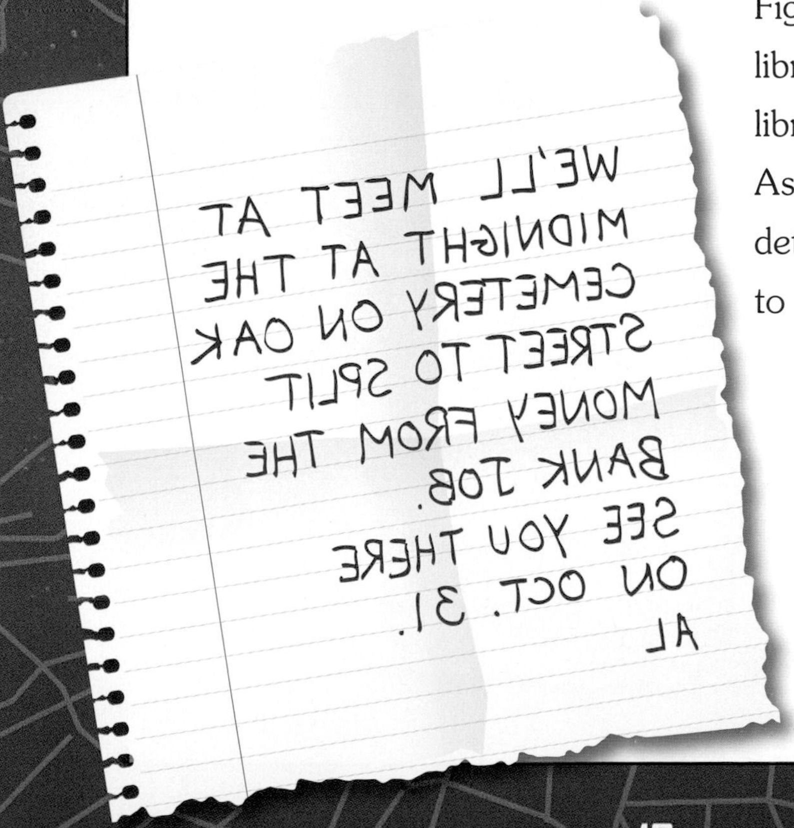

WE'LL MEET AT
MIDNIGHT AT THE
CEMETERY ON OAK
STREET TO SPLIT
MONEY FROM THE
BANK JOB.
SEE YOU THERE
ON OCT. 31.
AL

Figure 2. This note was given
to the police.

Seeing May Not Be Believing

A good detective knows she can be fooled by any of her senses (sight, hearing, touch, smell, and taste). Are you certain of everything you *see*? Are you sure about all that you hear or touch? Many people think they are. If you believe you are, you may change your mind after doing the experiments in this chapter.

2-1 Can You Believe All That You See?

1 Look carefully at the drawing in Figure 3a. Which line looks longer, the vertical or the horizontal?

THINGS YOU WILL NEED:
- Figure 3
- ruler

2 In Figure 3b, which vertical line looks longer?

3 Do you think the long, dark, slanted lines in Figure 3c are parallel?

4 Do you think the lines on the circles in Figure 3d are straight?

5 Use a ruler to carefully measure the lines in Figure 3a. How do their lengths compare?

How about the length of the lines in Figure 3b?

6 Carefully measure the distance between the long slanted lines in Figure 3c. Are the lines parallel?

7 In Figure 3d, hold a ruler up against each of the four lines. Are the lines straight?

a)

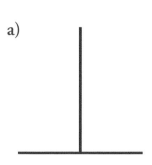

b)

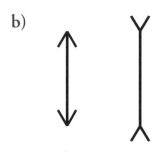

c)

d)

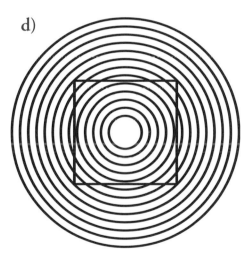

Figure 3a. Does one line look longer than the other?
    b. Does one of the vertical lines look longer? Is it longer?
    c. Do the long slanted lines look parallel? Are they parallel?
    d. Are the four lines inside the circles straight?

As you have seen, our eyes can be tricked. The drawings in Figure 3 are called illusions. They cause us to see things differently than they really are. This is one reason that eyewitness accounts may not be accurate.

Idea for a Science Fair Project

Design some illusions of your own. Use them to show people that they cannot believe everything they see.

2-2 The Color of Light Can Affect What We See

Detectives and eyewitnesses can make mistakes because of the light in which they see things. You will find that this is true by doing an experiment.

1 Find a room that can be made very dark. Remove the lightbulb from a lamp in that room. Replace the lightbulb with a red lightbulb. Turn off all other lights.

2 Hold an object you know to be green in the red light. What color does the object appear to be in red light? Can you explain why? If not, think about why a green object is green. (It is green because it reflects green light. If there is no green light, it reflects no light.)

3 Hold an object you know to be blue in the red light. What color does the object appear to be in red light? Can you explain why?

> **THINGS YOU WILL NEED:**
> - room that can be made totally dark
> - lamp
> - red lightbulb (available at the supermarket or hardware store)
> - green object
> - blue object

Ideas for Science Fair Projects

- Use red, green, and blue lightbulbs to produce light that is red, green, or blue. Examine different colored paper (red, green, blue, magenta, cyan, yellow, black, and white) in red light, in green light, and in blue light. Try to explain the color of each paper in each type of light.

- Use all three colored bulbs, alone and together, and a stick to produce colored shadows. How many shadows are produced by two colored lights? By three colored lights? What color are the shadows? Can you explain the color of each shadow you see?

- Sodium vapor streetlights emit yellow light. Observe cars under these yellow lights. How do their colors there compare with their colors in sunlight?

2-3 Can You Believe All That You Hear?

1 Have ten or more people sit in a circle. You will whisper a sentence to the person on your left. You might whisper, "Does the moon always rise shortly after the sun sets?"

2 The person on your left whispers what she heard to the person on her left.

3 This continues around the circle. Finally, the person on your right whispers what he has heard into your ear.

4 You then state out loud what was whispered to you. Then you repeat your original sentence.

How does what you whispered compare with what was whispered to you?

In courtrooms, judges will not allow hearsay evidence. Hearsay evidence is evidence a witness heard from someone else. Having done this experiment, do you think the judges are right?

THINGS YOU WILL NEED:
- 10 or more people
- a chair for each person, arranged in a large circle

Who Dunnit? A Crime to Solve: Hairs from a Crime Scene

A suspect has been arrested for murder. Hairs were found at the crime scene. The suspect's lawyer claims all the hairs are from the victim's head, so they are not the hairs of the suspect. You use a microscope to examine a hair from the victim's comb. What you see is shown in Figure 4a.

You then examine a hair found on the victim at the crime scene. What you see is shown in Figure 4b.

What do you conclude? Did both hairs come from the victim? What would you do next?

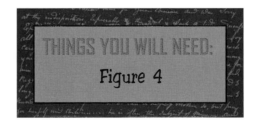

THINGS YOU WILL NEED:

Figure 4

 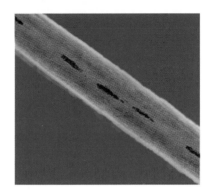

**Figure 4a. This hair from the victim's comb was magnified 640 times.
b. This hair found on the victim was magnified 640 times.**

Comparing Hairs Seen Through
a Comparison Microscope

Forensic scientists usually compare hair samples side by side under a comparison microscope. They look for many answers. Is the hair from a human or an animal? Do the hairs match in color, length, diameter, and other features inside the hair? Has the hair been bleached or colored? An expert may be able to tell from what part of the body the hair grew. It may also be possible to determine whether the hair is from an Asian, Caucasian, or African-American person.

Codes and Crime

3

Criminals, spies, and terrorists sometimes send coded messages. They would not use the Morse code of dots and dashes. It is much too common and well known. Detectives have to be able to think and reason like a scientist. If they discover coded messages, they have to try to break the code (figure it out).

In this chapter, you will examine some codes and invent your own code. Then you will try to solve a crime by breaking a code.

3-1 Using Codes to Communicate

Some examples of codes that might be used by criminals are shown in Table 1.

1 Invent a code of your own.

2 Write a message using your code. Give it to a friend or classmate. Can he or she decode it? Can you decode a message that your friend writes in his or her code?

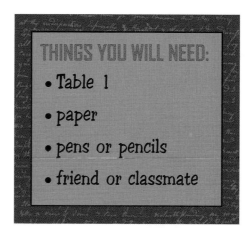

THINGS YOU WILL NEED:

- Table 1
- paper
- pens or pencils
- friend or classmate

Table 1: Some examples of codes

Example 1. A number represents a letter: 1 is A, 2 is B, 3 is C, . . . 24 is X, 25 is Y, 26 is Z.

Example 2. A number represents a letter, but in reverse order of Example 1: 26 is A, 25 is B, 24 is C, . . . 3 is X, 2 is Y, 1 is Z.

Continued on page 30

Continued from page 29

Example 3. Each letter is assigned two numbers. The first number is from a column, the second number is from a row. As shown below, A is 11, B is 21, C is 31, . . . X is 35, Y is 45, Z is 55. U and V are both 15.

	1	2	3	4	5
1	a	b	c	d	e
2	f	g	h	i	j
3	k	l	m	n	o
4	p	q	r	s	t
5	uv	w	x	y	z

Example 4. A message (hide the money) could be written in an up-down sequence like one of these:

H D   T E   M N Y or   HDTE MNY

I E   H   O E   IE H OE

Example 5. A simple code would be to write words in reverse order.

HIDE THE MONEY would be written as YENOM EHT EDIH.

Example 6. Messages could be written using mirror writing; that is the writing could be read by holding a mirror in front of it, as you learned in Experiment 1-4. Leonardo da Vinci's notebooks were written in this code.

Codes Used in World War II

During World War II (1939—1945), military messages were sent in code. American decoders broke the code of the Japanese Navy. They did so shortly after the Japanese attacked Pearl Harbor on December 7, 1941. As a result, the U.S. Navy surprised and destroyed a Japanese task force near Midway Island in June 1942.

The Japanese were not able to break the U.S. Marines' code. The marines hired Navajos to send messages. These Native Americans simply spoke in a modified form of their unwritten native language. They were known as Navajo Code Talkers. Their code was never broken.

← These men are training in California to be Navajo Code Talkers.

These Navajo Code Talkers send a coded message → from the South Pacific using a field radio in 1943.

Who Dunnit? A Crime to Solve: Breaking a Code

THINGS YOU WILL NEED:

Figure 5

On Monday, a police officer on street duty found a note. The note was just a series of numbers. The note is shown in Figure 5.

The police suspected the numbers were a code. As an expert on codes, you are called to headquarters to examine the note. Can you decode the message? If you can, what will you suggest the police do?

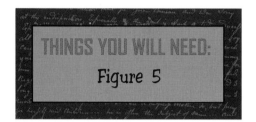

25 22   26 7   7 19 22   14 26 18 13   8 7 9 22 22 7

25 26 13 16   26 7   13 18 13 22   7 12 14 12 9 9 12 4

4 22 23 13 22 8 23 26 2   11 26 9 16   7 19 22   24 26 9

12 13   12 26 16   8 7 9 22 22 7

Figure 5. The police found this note on the street.

Not So Smart Criminals

Not all criminals are smart enough to invent or use codes. Some make really dumb errors. In 1995, a man was arrested for an armed robbery in New Jersey. During the robbery, he used a piece of thin cardboard to wedge a door open. When police removed the wedge, they discovered it was a traffic ticket. On the ticket were the robber's name and address. Police had no trouble finding the robber.

In another case, a hitchhiker robbed the person who had given him a ride. When he got home, he discovered the wallet he had stolen was empty. But his wallet, which contained his name and address, was missing. He had left it in the car with the man he had robbed.

4

Detectives and Eyewitness Evidence

Someone who sees a crime take place is called an eyewitness. That person may be asked to tell the police what he or she saw. What that person reports is called eyewitness evidence. Eyewitness evidence is all some juries need to convict someone of a crime.

Detectives have become less willing to accept eyewitness reports of a crime. Eyewitness reports are based on memory, and memories fade with time. Memories are swayed by emotions, thoughts, and feelings during the crime. They can also be affected by newspaper and television reports about the crime.

Crimes often occur quickly. They may take place at night under poor lighting. A clear view of the criminal may not be possible. Crimes are stressful, so a witness may not be focused on the criminal or details connected to the crime.

To reduce eyewitness errors, detectives try to reach the eyewitnesses as soon as possible. They first ask each witness to tell his or her story without interruption. Then they ask specific questions to probe the witness's memory.

If a suspect is arrested, the witness can be asked to view a lineup. A lineup is a row of individuals. One of the people in the row is the suspect. The other people who are there resemble the suspect as much as possible.

4-1 Can You Remember All That You See?

1 Place about a dozen objects on a tray. You might include such things as a comb, a pen, paper clips, an eraser, beads, chalk, crayons, a pencil, a sock, a slipper, a lightbulb, a photograph, or other things you have available.

2 Cover the tray and contents with a large towel or cloth.

3 Ask someone to stand near the tray. Tell him or her that you are going to remove the cover for ten seconds. (Many crimes take place in ten seconds or less.) That person is to observe the uncovered tray for ten seconds.

4 After ten seconds, cover the tray again.

THINGS YOU WILL NEED:

- about a dozen objects such as a comb, pen, paper clips, eraser, beads, chalk, crayons, pencil, sock, slipper, lightbulb, photograph
- tray
- large towel or cloth
- several people
- pencil
- paper

5 Hand the person a pencil and a sheet of paper. Ask him or her to write down the names of the things that were on the tray.

How many things did the person remember? Did he or she "remember" anything that was not there?

6 Repeat the experiment with a number of different people.

Do people remember all that they see?

Ideas for Science Fair Projects

• Do girls remember more of what they see than boys? Do experiments to find out.

• Do children remember more of what they see than adults? Do experiments to find out.

• Interrupt the observer with a blast of loud music by turning on a radio or stereo for five of the ten seconds. Does the "stress" of the loud music make it harder for people to remember what they see?

4-2 Eyewitnesses to a "Crime"

1 Ask your teacher for permission to stage a mock (fake) crime. Tell him or her that you are doing an experiment. You want to see how well eyewitnesses remember a crime scene.

(With your parent's permission, you could do a similar experiment at a family gathering.)

THINGS YOU WILL NEED:

- teacher's permission
- parent, friend, or older brother or sister to be the "criminal"
- clock or watch
- wallet, CD, another watch, or something else of value
- classmates
- papers with the questions shown in Figure 6

2 Arrange to have a parent, a friend, or an older brother or sister be the "criminal."

3 Set a time for the crime that is agreeable to you, your teacher, and the "criminal."

4 Plan to be away from your desk at the time of the "crime." Leave something of value on your desk. It might be a wallet, a CD, a watch, or something else. Be sure the "criminal" knows where your desk is located.

Questions for Eyewitnesses to a Crime

1. Describe what you saw.

2. Was the robber male or female?

3. Approximately how tall was the "robber"?

4. Approximately how much do you think the person weighed?

5. What was the person's hair color?
   Was it straight or curly? Long or short?

6. What was the person's eye color?

7. What was the person's skin color?

8. Describe what the person was wearing.

9. What did the person remove from the room?

10. What else do you remember?

Figure 6. These are some possible questions for eyewitnesses to a "crime."

5 The "criminal" will boldly open the door and look around the room. He or she will walk to your desk and take the thing of value. After looking around the room again, the "criminal" will leave.

6 After the "crime," hand each person who saw the crime a sheet of paper. They are the eyewitnesses. The paper should have the questions shown in Figure 6. (You can use a copier to make copies of Figure 6. DO NOT WRITE IN THIS BOOK!) Ask the eyewitnesses to answer the questions based on what they saw.

7 Collect their answers and compare them. Do all the eyewitnesses agree?

8 A week later, hand out the questions again. How well do they remember what happened? How does time affect people's memory of an event?

What can you conclude, if anything, about eyewitnesses?

Ideas for a Science Fair Project

- Extend Experiment 4-2. Gather a number of photographs of people. One of the photographs should be of the "criminal." Use these photos as what police call mug shots. See if eyewitnesses can identify the criminal among a "lineup" of mug shots.

- Some people claim that they can identify a criminal just by looking at his or her face. Gather photographs—from newspapers, magazines, and other sources—of people who are proven criminals and people (not famous) who are not criminals to make a "lineup." Then test as many people as possible. Can anyone consistently identify the criminals?

Who Dunnit? A Crime to Solve: Mistaken Identity

1 Police have investigated a fictional "murder." A "suspect" has been arrested. A video camera at the crime scene recorded the "murderer's" face. The video picture has been enhanced by a police computer. The "murderer's" photograph is shown in Figure 7.

2 The suspect's DNA matches that in a hair found at the crime scene. However, the suspect has an alibi. He claims he was at a party at the time of the murder. People at the party have backed his story.

3 The police ask you to investigate. You photograph the "suspect" (see Figure 8).

4 You compare the two photographs and question the "suspect."

5 You tell the police they have arrested the wrong man. You then tell them whom to arrest. What do you tell them?

THINGS YOU WILL NEED:

- Figure 7
- Figure 8

Figure 7. This is an enhanced video photograph of the fictional murderer.

Figure 8. This is a photograph of the fictional suspect.

Answers

Figure 1: The safe is open. What looks like paper money lies in front of the safe. A snowman can be seen through the window on the left. The window on the right is open even though it is winter. There is a footprint beneath the open window. There are some red drops on the floor and on the open window that could be blood. The picture on the wall is askew. A wastebasket has been tipped over. A drawer has been removed from the desk. On the desk, a cup has been tipped over and what may be coffee has spilled. The phone is off the hook, and the phone line has been cut. A broken chair is in front of the left window.

The open safe, paper money, open window, footprint, possible blood, tilted picture, spilled wastebasket, removal of desk drawer, spilled coffee, phone off the hook, and cut phone line all suggest a crime has been committed.

Evidence you should look for and collect: fingerprints on safe, phone, window, cup, desk drawers, wastebasket, picture; samples of bloodstains; photograph of the footprint.

Experiment 1-4: When the paper is held in front of a mirror, the note can be read. It says, "We'll meet at midnight at the cemetery on Oak Street to split money from the bank job. See you there on Oct. 31. [Signed] Al

You realize this is probably the money from the bank that was robbed on October 28. You arrange to have police hiding in the cemetery on October 31 (Halloween), wait for the robbers to split the money, and then arrest them.

Experiment 2-4: The hairs do not match. Both hairs did not belong to the victim. The next step would be to examine hair from the suspect under a microscope. If it matches the hair found on the victim, the next step would be to compare DNA from the hair with DNA from the suspect.

Experiment 3-2: The message is: BE AT THE MAIN STREET BANK AT NINE TOMORROW, WEDNESDAY, PARK THE CAR ON OAK STREET. Each letter is represented by a number. A is 26, B is 25, . . . Y is 2, Z is 1. You should tell the police to be at the bank and car to intercept the bank robbers.

Experiment 4-3: You tell them to arrest the suspect's identical twin. Because the men are identical twins, they have the same DNA. However, they are not quite identical. Look at the photographs carefully. They are not of the same person. The mole on the suspect's face and on the face from the video are on different parts of their faces.

Words to Know

code—Letters, symbols, numbers, or words used to represent words in messages that only the receiver can decode and understand.

comparison microscope—An instrument that combines the enlarged images of objects seen through two microscopes. The two objects can be compared by viewing them side by side.

crime scene—The place where a crime happened.

decode—To convert a coded message into one that can be read and understood.

evidence—Things that can be used to solve crimes and to convict criminals in a court of law, such as fingerprints, hair, blood, etc.

eyewitness—A person who has seen something such as a crime.

forensic science—The science used to investigate and solve crimes. It is also used in courts of law.

forensic scientist—A person who uses science to solve crimes and whose findings may be used as evidence in court.

microscope—An instrument that uses lenses to magnify (increase the apparent size of) an object.

Further Reading

Bardhan-Quallen, Sudipta. *Championship Science Fair Projects: 100 Sure-To-Win Experiments.* New York: Sterling, 2004.

Bochinski, Julianne Blair. *The Complete Workbook for Science Fair Projects.* New York: John Wiley and Sons, 2005.

Clemson, Wendy and David, Kev Prichard, and Dr. Allison Jones. *Using Math to Solve a Crime.* Milwaukee: Gareth Stevens Publishing, 2005.

Fridell, Ron. *Forensic Science.* Minneapolis: Lerner Publications Company, 2007.

Hopping, Lorraine Jean. *Crime Scene Science: Investigating a Crime Scene.* Milwaukee: World Almanac Library, 2007.

Pentland, Peter, and Pennie Stoyles. *Forensic Science.* Philadelphia: Chelsea House Publishers, 2003.

Internet Addresses

Access Excellence. *The Mystery Spot.*
www.accessexcellence.org/AE/mspot/

F.B.I. Youth.
www.fbi.gov/kids/6th12th/6th12th.htm

Who Dunnit?
http://www.cyberbee.com/whodunnit/crime.html

Index